LET'S TALK ABOUT
FEELING DEFEATED

Joy Berry

Let's Talk About Feeling Defeated

Copyright ©2013 by Joy Berry
All Rights Reserved.

Published by Inspired Studios, Inc.
11924 Forest Hill Blvd.
Ste. 10A-298
Wellington, FL 33414

Published under license from Brite Star Media Group, Inc.

ISBN
Softcover   978-0-7396-0223-2
Digital   978-0-7396-0224-9

Hello, my name is Bouncer.

I'd like to tell you a story about my friend, Lennie.

Sometimes Lennie loses when he competes with someone.

Lennie feels defeated.

Feeling defeated is feeling put down.

Feeling defeated is feeling like a loser.

Sometimes feeling defeated can cause you to feel discouraged.

You might feel as though you are never going to succeed or win.

Remembering these facts will help you to feel better when you feel defeated.

- No one succeeds at everything.
- Everyone fails at one time or another.
- No one wins all of the time.
- Everyone loses some of the time.

Remembering these facts can help you to feel better when you feel defeated.

- No one is perfect, including you.
- Like every other person, you are probably going to fail once in a while.
- Like every other person, you are probably going to lose once in a while.

Try not to feel badly about yourself when you fail or lose.

Do not believe that you are a loser.

Do not believe that you will never win.

Try not to give up when you fail or lose.

It is important to keep trying, because the more you try, the more you increase your chances of winning.

If trying hard is not enough, do something to make yourself better at what you are attempting to do.

- Learn more about what you are doing.
- Ask other people to teach you.
- Watch other people, and learn from the way that they do things.

Once you have learned everything you need to know, practice.

Practice is doing something over and over again until you can do it well.

Obviously, you've been practicing!

Sometimes you might continue to lose after you have done all that you can do to win. Do something else if you continue to lose. It will help if you realize that losing often can mean that:

- you are not ready to do what you are trying to do.
- what you are trying to do is something you should not do at this time.

Try to turn your failures and losses into positive experiences.

You can learn valuable lessons whenever you fail or lose.

You can learn what you should and should not do in order to win.

You can also learn how to treat other people when they lose.

Remember that everyone feels defeated at one time or another.

So, do not feel ashamed about feeling defeated.

Instead, do things that will make you feel better whenever you feel defeated.

CPSIA information can be obtained
at www.ICGtesting.com
Printed in the USA
BVHW051518140819
555665BV00059B/3423/P

9 780739 602232